FORGOTT
LANDSCAPE

images of Pendle Hill, the Ribble Valley and the Burnley area

alastair lee

FORGO
LAND

images of Pendle Hill, the Ri

published by Pos

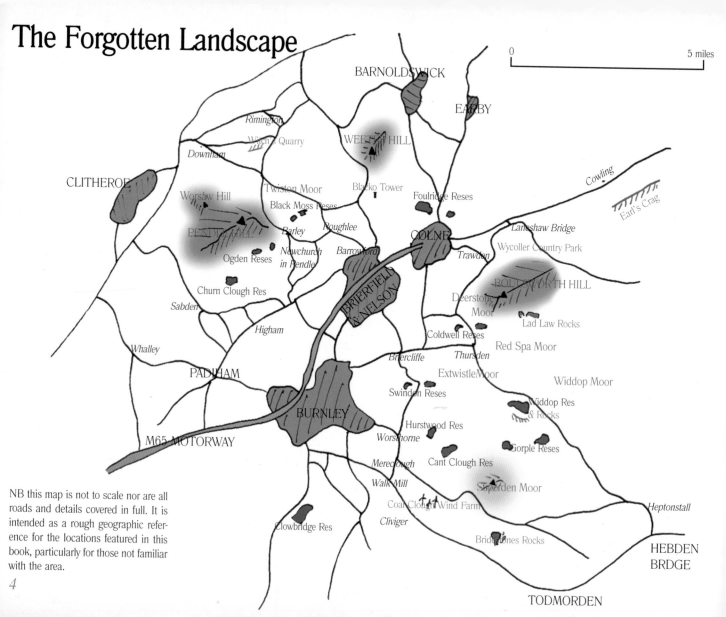

The Forgotten Landscape

0   5 miles

BARNOLDSWICK

EARBY

Rimington

Witch's Quarry

WEETS HILL

Downham

Blacko Tower

Cowling

CLITHEROE

Twiston Moor

Foulridge Reses

Earl's Crag

Worsaw Hill

Black Moss Reses

Laneshaw Bridge

Wycoller Country Park

PENDLE HILL

Barley

Roughlee

COLNE

Ogden Reses

Newchurch in Pendle

Barrowford

Trawden

BOULSWORTH HILL

Churn Clough Res

BRIERFIELD & NELSON

Deerstones Moor

Lad Law Rocks

Sabden

Coldwell Reses

Red Spa Moor

Higham

Thursden

Whalley

Briercliffe

Extwistle Moor

Widdop Moor

PADIHAM

Swinden Reses

Widdop Res & Rocks

Hurstwood Res

Gorple Reses

BURNLEY

Worsthorne

Cant Clough Res

M65 MOTORWAY

Mereclough

Shedden Moor

Walk Mill

Heptonstall

Coal Clough Wind Farm

Clowbridge Res

Cliviger

Bride Stones Rocks

HEBDEN BRDGE

TODMORDEN

NB this map is not to scale nor are all roads and details covered in full. It is intended as a rough geographic reference for the locations featured in this book, particularly for those not familiar with the area.

4

Contents

TITLE PAGE - A gritstone rock-pool on Lad Law Rocks behind Boulsworth Hill, Pendle Borough.
PREVIOUS PAGE - Patchwork fields of Pendle Borough, as seen from Earl's Crag near Cowling.

Pendle Hill & Ogden Clough near Barley, Pendle Borough.

Forgotten landscape? Well never by myself or the countless other enthusiasts who appreciate the marvellous countryside surrounding the Burnley, Pendle and Clitheroe area. Whether walking, fishing, shooting, climbing, horseriding, biking, skiing, paragliding, canoeing or flying a remote controlled plane there is a great bond between the local community and the Forgotten Landscape.

Forgotten then by whom? On a national scale, the Forgotten Landscape is perhaps not so much forgotten, rather, never even known! Lying to the south is the UK's first and busiest national park; The Peak District, whilst to the north we lay in the shadows of the tourist rich Yorkshire Dales National Park and The Lake District, admittedly three stunning areas. Perhaps there is a sense of irony within the title 'Forgotten Landscape', in that this body of work is here to remind us of the great landscapes which we are bound by, hence the message is not to forget the landscape and the spiritual value it holds.

There is a third interpretation of the title which is perhaps of a more abstract nature which could be applied more generally to any landscape. As you begin to look through the images within this book you will notice that they are not all wide panoramic scenes, there is plenty of focus on the smaller details that make up the landscape, microcosms of beauty that pull on the old adage, 'less is invariably more'.

One of the great pleasures of roaming through this landscape is how quickly you can feel isolated and grasp the inner peace of solitude, in comparison with the masses that clog up the Peak District's winding roads or polish the steps at Malham Cove in the Yorkshire Dales. In many ways I hope the charm of the Forgotten Landscape remains a 'secret garden' for its immediate inhabitants, not gaining the levels of popularity that other tourist 'honeypots' have reached. This book is intended for those who, like myself, know of the great diversity and excellent locations around the Burnley, Clitheroe and Pendle areas. It is intended for all to enjoy and celebrate the landscape, a tomb to cherish on the bookshelf or send abroad to proudly show friends and family the area where you live.

Introduction

As a child, walks up Pendle Hill from Barley were frequent and during my upbringing in Brierfield adventures in the nearby fields, brooks and clay-pits were an intergral part of my own mental and physical development. Open spaces, muddy boots, rivers, woods, grazed knees and steep hills are all features which I'm grateful I've never had to live without *(okay I don't graze my knees so much these days!)*. However, like many people my conception of living in Lancashire was one of grey skies, slate roofs, tall chimneys and pessimistic gloom. It wasn't until I'd left home to travel around the world that I really began to appreciate the area where I'd always lived.

ABOVE LEFT - As seen at Wycoller, Pendle Borough. ABOVE RIGHT - Walkers on the Nick o' Pendle.

Perhaps familiarity breeds contempt, or you don't appreciate what you have until its gone, as the saying goes, or perhaps my sense for aesthetics was beginning to mature. Either way over the past ten years I have been infected by an unrelenting passion for the local landscape and continually discover new miniature worlds of beauty and find fresh perspectives of familiar views.

In this book I have tried to include all the popular sights from the specified area (ie Pendle, Ribble Valley and Burnley) however there are bound to be some great scenes that have been omitted. For this I apologise. There is also an inevitable bias towards my own favourite places. For example the steep hills of Pendle and Boulsworth (the two most significant landmarks in the area) and also the rock climbing areas of Widdop, Bridestones and Earl's Crag, as I am a keen rock climber and visit these locations on a weekly, if not, daily basis.

The landscapes covered in this book do not strictly coincide with the official borough boundaries either. As many areas, like Widdop Reservoir for example although just within The Borough of Calderdale is in fact closer to Briercliffe just outside the town of Burnley than Heptonstall the nearest village in Calderdale. In effect, I have ignored both borough and county boundaries using the perspective that if a location is considered to be 'local' then it is a valid inclusion for the Forgotten Landscape (see map on page 4 for exact locations).

ABOVE - Waymarker for the Pendle Way, Pendle Borough.
RIGHT - Trees in the mist, Mereclough, Burnley Borough.
OPPOSITE - A storm breaks over the Ribble Valley, as seen from Downham Moor.

It should also be pointed out that the Forgotten Landscape's primary focus, as you may expect, is about what occurs naturally. Therefore there is little visual reference to the area's famous industrial history. For pictures of canals, horse-drawn carts and mills I suggest you purchase one of the many publications that cover this topic. There is however an unavoidable reference to man's interaction and influence upon the landscape, from drystone walls and cattle to wind farms and reservoirs. Although the popular notion of man and the environment is a critical one, there are some cases where the benefits undeniably outway the negative aspects. With that in mind my view of the alteration humans have made to the Fogotten Landscape is a positive one. I see farming and reservoirs not so much as conquering or damaging the landscape, rather, having respect for it and finding some level of harmony with the landscape.

I have kept the categorization in the book quite simple, the reason for this is that the main focus of this book is the images captured in the specified area, beyond that this book is not intended to extensively cover every listed reservoir or tree species in existence. The combination of my enthusiasm for this landscape with my artistic input through photography will hopefully demonstrate what a stunning place the Forgotten Landscape can be.

"The earth laughs in flowers." Ralph Waldo Emerson (1803-1882) from *Hamatreya.*

Flora

woodlands, flowers and grasses

FORGOTTEN
LANDSCAPE
Images of Pendle Hill, the Ribble Valley and the Burnley area

Snowdrops on the forest floor in a small wood between Hurstwood and Cliviger, Burnley Borough.
ABOVE - An oak tree in winter, Cliviger.

With the world talking of global warming and deforestation, it seems an appropriate time to pay attention to, and acknowledge the plantlife in our immediate environment. A look back in history reveals that much of the English landscape was once forested before the advent of modern agriculture. The earliest settlers in this area took to the highground on the moors as the valleys were simply too vegetated to inhabit. The industrial revolution (17th - 19th centuries) was to change all that as the valleys became densely populated areas due to their damp climate being so ideally suited for the spinning of cotton.

The present day landscape is rich with vegetation and there is hope for the future as massive broadleaf tree planting operations are undertaken in the Burnley area *(I can personally guarantee the sound planting of a few thousand of the aforementioned trees!)*. First growth trees and plantations which remain should be treated as treasured plots on the landscape.

ABOVE - Gorse bush blooming in the springtime, found throughout the area. This one is near Noggarth, Pendle Borough. BELOW - Windswept hawthorne tree, Nick o'Pendle, Ribble Valley.

There is a great diversity of species in the area from the grandeur of an oak to a busy birch or hawthorne and elegance of an ash. Many take pride of place in a garden, line the driveway to an estate or divide the farmland providing a habitat for tawny & long-eared owls, foxes and other types of fauna. Often the most exciting areas to visit for those seeking wooded vegetation are the babbling brooks, which in many cases remain untouched, as the mosses and deadwood which encave the rivers and streams testify.

Broadleaf tree planting at Clowbridge Reservoir, Burnley Borough.

Flora

woodlands, flowers and grasses

The Forgotten Landscape is not an area that you would immediately associate with forests. When one studies an Ordnance Survey map however there are areas marked 'Forest of Trawden' and 'Forest of Pendle' yet an investigation into these areas reveals no great expanse of woodland as one might expect. These terms are still used from old hunting terminology where the word 'forest' would simply mean 'hunting ground'. Having stated that in taking on this project, I have come to realise just how many pockets of trees and wooded boundaries exist in the area, once you begin to look. The most popular and extensive forests to be found at the moment however are the relatively new pine forests (mainly conifers) planted in the '60s and '70s which can be found on farmland across the area.

There are also great numbers of other plantlife to be found around Burnley and Pendle; heather, lavender sphagnum and yellow mosses, bracken and grasses on the moors, snowdrops on the forest floor, gorse and foxgloves in the valleys and daffodils by the river bank, ahh.... The book begins with a selection of images of the flora from this area. Having always been a bit of a tree hugger there is a slight emphasis on the fantastic trees, providing oxygen, a habitat for birds, and more importantly, a source for grand aesthetics!

Bracken sharp, bracken blurred, from Earl's Crag, Pendle Hill in background.

13

FORGOTTEN

images of Pendle Hill, the Ribble Valley and the Burnley area

LANDSCAPE

360 degree view from inside Thursden Forest situated just off Widdop Road, Pendle Borough.

FORGOTTEN LANDSCAPE

Images of Pendle Hill, the Ribble Valley and the Burnley area

Trees and moss on the
River Brun, running
through the Hurstwood
area. Burnley Borough.
Continued overleaf......

An elegant and exotic tree at sunset, Worsthorne, Burnley Borough.

Tussock grass in the snow Twiston Moor near Pendle Hill, Pendle Borough.

Tree bark and moss found at the base of Worsaw Hill, Ribble Valley.

Dead bracken buried in the snow on the eastern slopes of Pendle Hill, Pendle Borough.

Grass, Hurstwood Resovoir, Burnley Borough.

OPPOSITE - Forest floor view of the tree tops of Thursden Forest, Pendle Borough.

Tussock grass, near Barley, Pendle Borough - Daffodils by the River Brun, Hurstwood, Burnley Borough.
OPPOSITE - Foxgloves on the moors, Pendle Borough.

PREVIOUS PAGE - an oak tree at sunset near Newchurch in Pendle, Pendle Borough.

Mossy rocks and trees from the River Brun, Burnley Borough. There are many untouched woods and rivers waiting to be discovered where mosses and lichens thrive in the damp, unpolluted climate.

FROM TOP LEFT ANTICLOCKWISE - An ash tree in winter off Halifax Road, Nelson, Pendle Borough - Birch trees at sunset off Clitheroe Rd, near Sabden, Ribble Valley - Ribble Valley trees in a summer haze, Ribble Valley - Morning shadows from Barley, Pendle Borough - Hawthorne tree on Worsaw Hill, Ribble Valley.

FORGOTTEN
LANDSCAPE
Images of Pendle Hill, the Ribble Valley and the Burnley area

Scots pine plantation at the foot of Pendle Hill, Ribble Valley.

'Trees that walk' near Sabden, Ribble Valley Borough. There can't be a better argument that it was in fact the landscape around Tolkien that helped inspire the classic 'Lord of the Rings' book. Tolkien lived at Stoneyhurst College, Ribble Valley, when the book was written.

A line of energetic birch trees on a moody evening, 'The Water Meetings' Barrowford, Pendle Borough.

Snowdrops blooming in February, found in a small forest between Hurstwood and Cliviger, Burnley Borough.

A beech tree verdant in mid-summer with Pendle Hill behind as seen near Rimington, Ribble Valley.

The same scene as opposite, this time on a cold evening in January.

Birch trees at sunset on a farm near Hurstwood, Burnley Borough.

Oak trees at sunset from Clitheroe Road near Sabden, Ribble Valley.

"I love Pendle Hill and from whatever side I view it, whether from Whalley, where I see it from end to end, from its lowest point to its highest: from Padiham where it frowns upon me; from Clitheroe where it smiles; or from Downham, where it rises in full majesty before me - from all its points and under all aspects, whether robed with mist or radient with sunshine, I delight in it." - HARRISON AINSWORTH, from *Pendle Hill in History and Literature* by James Mckay F.R.H.S.(1888).

Pendle Hill

and its views

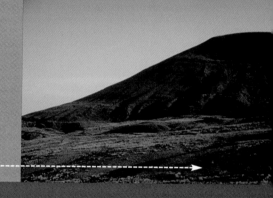

FORGOTTEN
Images of Pendle Hill, the Ribble Valley and the Burnley area
LANDSCAPE

Pendle Hill with a dusting of snow early morning in May.
ABOVE - The 'Big End' as seen from Downham, Ribble Valley.

For many people Pendle Hill signifies home more than any other landmark. This hill and all of its 557m in height above sea level is one of Lancashire's most famous 'lumps' in the landscape. The hill is steeped in myth and legend from witchcraft to divine inspiration. In 1612, nine people from Pendle were hanged for witchcraft in Lancaster, including Alice Nutter whose grave can be found in Newchurch in Pendle, Pendle. Then forty-one years later in 1653 George Fox climbed Pendle Hill resulting in a vision, which lead to the foundation of the Quaker movement. Four hundred years on and Pendle Hill's empowering allure has grown massively in popularity as it is the area's foremost hiking destination and one of the country's top paragliding locations. Witches on brooms, men hanging from fluorescent sails in the sky....... I'm not accusing anybody of possession with supernatural powers, however there is a certain irony in the air!

LEFT - Pendle Hill basking in the soft light of a late summer's evening.
BELOW - The Nick o'Pendle (Pendleton Moor) from Clitheroe Road, Ribble Valley.

The distinctive shape of Pendle Hill is recognizable from miles around, the slight hump back and dramatic steep slopes of the 'Big End' are the features that make the arcane beauty of Pendle so unmistakable from afar. The peaks of Pen-y-Ghent and Ingleborough in the Yorkshire Dales to the north are easily viewed in all but the worst conditions from the vantage point this magnificent hill offers. On a very clear day the Langdale Pikes in the Lake District some fifty miles north and west can be viewed, as can Blackpool Tower and the Irish Sea, in the right light.

Although the hill's height is modest (actually only 169ft short of being classified as a mountain), the views from its summit are impressive. The reason for this is the lack of any other hills of a similar height within the immediate vicinity. Within the Pennines (the backbone of the UK), Pendle Hill reigns unique as far as isolated peaks are concerned. The landscape on all sides of the hill drops away to 100m or less before another hill of a similar height is encountered, (in this case Boulsworth at 517m). Directly to the east, the next piece of land of a similar height to Pendle Hill is some 2700 miles away; The Russian Steppes! *(Ural Mountains.)*

For me the hill embodies all that is great about a good landscape. The same feature can have so many different appearances from different angles in the varying conditions of each year. I have climbed the hill over 100 times and still look forward to the next time I reach the summit again. Perhaps the most intriguing facet about Pendle Hill is the many different appearences the Hill takes on from different sides which are so clearly viewed due to its isolated nature. My favourite view is from the Middop area, off Gisburn Rd where it takes on a uniform symmetrical appearance (see page 51). Which is your favourite angle??

ABOVE LEFT - Bags of stones delivered by helicopter to replace Pendle's main path.
BELOW - The hill in winter wonderland attire, February.

FORGOTTEN
images of Pendle Hill, the Ribble Valley and the Burnley area
LANDSCAPE

180 degree view of Pendle Hill from the road between Roughlee and Downham, early on a spring morning, Pendle Borough.

PREVIOUS PAGE - When viewed from the east and north Pendle Hill takes on a quite symmetrical appearance, as seen from Middop near Rimington, Ribble Valley. Who needs Ayers Rock!
ABOVE - Looking over the verdant Ribble Valley in summer from Pendle Hill's 'Big End'.

Endless views from Pendle's main path over the rain shadow in winter conditions.

FORGOTTEN LANDSCAPE

Images of Pendle Hill, the Ribble Valley and the Bristlecone

Ogden stream on the summit plateau of Pendle Hill.

OPPOSITE - sunset from the summit of Pendle Hill - Sunset over Pendle Hill as seen from Lomeshaye Rd, Nelson - Drystone wall at the base of Pendle glowing at sunset - Pendle Hill in a spring haze as seen from the moors - Sunset over the Trough of Bowland from Pendle Hill.

A snow storm clears from Pendle Hill's 'Big End' in March, Pendle Borough.

CLOCKWISE FROM TOP LEFT - Blacko Tower at sunrise (5:30am) in May, as seen from Pendle Hill - Pendle 'robed in mist' as seen from Worsthorne, Burnley Borough - Pastoral lands lead to Pendle Hill as seen from Earl's Crag - Cloudburst at sunrise over Weetes Hill, as seen from Pendle Hill.

LEFT - The hill in evening light from Witch's Quarry, Ribble Valley.
ABOVE - Dramatic storm clouds over the Ribble Valley, as seen from Downham Moor.

OPPOSITE - Rare conditions as the urban corridor of Colne, Nelson and Burnley lies in a thick blanket
of fog as seen from Pendle Hill's summit.
ABOVE - Looking down the eastern slope of Pendle Hill in winter.

Footprints on a snow covered summit plateau - The upper eastern slopes of Pendle Hill in alpine conditions.

A covering of snow highlights two of Pendle's geological features; a large clough and the 'Big End'.

360 degree panorama of Pendle Hill looking across Downham Moor, Ribble Valley. One of the most dramatic viewpoints as the vertical scale from this outlook covers 250m to the summit.

Hikers on the summit plateau of Pendle Hill enjoying the spectacular conditions of a cloud-inversion.

CLOCKWISE - Bog trotting across Downham Moor - Approaching the top from the 'Big End' - Mist creeps over the Hill
- Pendle's triangulation point.

Downham village in the mist, as seen from Pendle's summit, Ribble Valley.
OPPOSITE - Above the cloudline on a foggy March morning from Pendle Hill.

High altitude cirrus clouds preceding a storm over Pendle.

'Sleeping Pendle' at dusk in autumn as seen from Pen-y-Ghent in the Yorkshire Dales.

The sun breaks through a showery evening in April, Pendle Hill and Downham Moor, Ribble Valley.

"*My love for Heathcliff resembles the eternal rocks beneath:- a source of little visible delight, but necessary.*" Emily Brontë (1818-1848) *taken from* **Wuthering Heights.**

The Moors

big skies, rocks, ruins and peat bogs

FORGOTTEN
Images of Pendle Hill, the Ribble Valley and the Burnley area
LANDSCAPE

'I wondered lonely as a..........', Worsthorne Moor as seen from Long Causeway, Burnley Borough.
ABOVE - Only the doorway remains from a 15th century church, Red Spa Moor, Pendle Borough.

The high moorlands to the south east of the Pendle Hill area offer a very different type of landscape of a much vaster perspective. The depths of the lush valleys and rolling green hills are left behind. By contrast, these windtorn gritstone plateaus have a bleak, wide and wild atmosphere.

Gritstone outcrops and boulders lay strewn across the barren curves of the moors; eroded by the wind and rain the rocks stand like sculptures from nature that any artist would struggle to compete with: testament to the raw beauty found on the moorlands. The rocks found at the Bridestones, Widdop and Earl's Crag offer some of the best 'bouldering' in the country and are popular with local and visiting climbers alike. *(Bouldering: an established sport, involves free climbing boulders of up to 5m in height with the use of a 'spotter' or landing pad for protection).*

There is often an eerie feel when walking amongst the many abandoned enclosure walls from mining settlements gone by, the ruins of Gorple Village from the copper-mines in the 18th century are a good example. However, the natural resource that modern man is beginning to harness is not quarried sandstone, lime or metals mined from beneath the ground but something very powerful in the air; the wind. Designated as one of the windiest places in the UK, Worsthorne Moor just outside of Burnley is home to a twenty-four turbine windfarm, providing 9.6 megawatts of power. *(A nuclear power station provides 1000MW).*

Bitter exposure is something you will become akin with on the moors, yet wildlife persists with red grouse, pheasants, kestrels, rabbits, weasels and deer who survive on this harsh landmass. Although one thing that is unlikely to be in short supply on the moorland is water, the moors as good as they look in the sunshine can often be an extremely wet place. Visibility becomes poor as the mist meets the skyline and the many reservoirs, tarns and bogs all get a good top up!

The Moors

big skies, rocks, ruins and peat bogs

There is much to be discovered on the moors, from ancient stone circles, World War II lookout bunkers and ruins, to the heights of Boulsworth Hill at 517m just 40m lower than Pendle Hill. There is a special beauty to the subtleties of the moors where the high average relief presents a big sky feel. Stiperden and Worsthorne Moors have been designated as a special site of scientific interest with rare plantlife and nesting curlew, redshank and lapwing birds in the spring time.

I hope this section of the book inspires you to get out onto what is ultimately an impressive and unique part of the landscape where many hidden delights await to be discovered.

TOP LEFT - Cotton grass as seen on Stiperden Moor, Burnley Borough. LEFT - Shooting posts, Widdop Moor. TOP RIGHT - The ruins of Robin Hood's House on route for Lad Law Rocks, Pendle Borough. RIGHT - Coal Clough Windfarm, Burnley Borough.

FORGOTTEN
LANDSCAPE
images of Pendle Hill, the Ribble Valley and the Burnley area

360 degree panorama of Lad Law Rocks on the borough boundary between Pendle and Calderdale, Boulsworth Hill is behind the large free-standing boulder to the left.

ABOVE - Big skies over Red Spa Moor, Pendle Borough - Abandoned enclosure wall, Stiperden Moor, Burnley Borough - Deerstone Moor near Boulsworth, Pendle Borough.
OPPOSITE - Frozen peat bogs, Hurstwood, Burnley Borough.

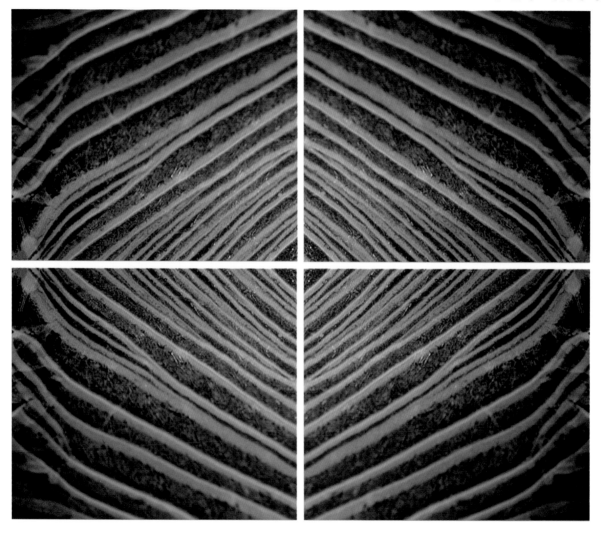

FORGOTTEN
images of Pendle Hill, the Ribble Valley and the Burnley area
LANDSCAPE

The Bridestone or the 'Egg', Bridestone Moor
437m, Calderdale Borough.

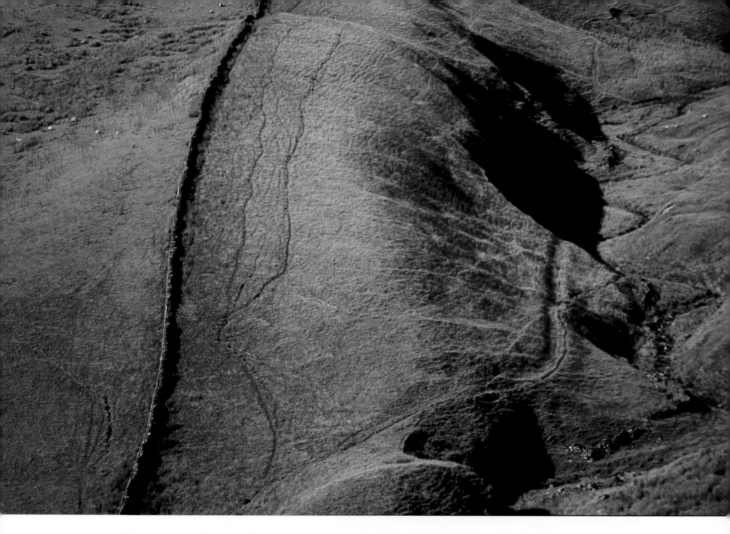

The meandering Thursden Brook and a drystone wall climbs steeply up the moorside, Pendle Borough.
OPPOSITE - Double exposure of the setting sun over Extwistle Moor, Pendle Borough.
Ice patterns of a frozen bog, Hurstwood, Burnley Borough.

FORGOTTEN
LANDSCAPE

images of Pendle Hill, the Ribble valley and the Trough of Bowland

The magnificent Cave Buttress, found overlooking the dam at Widdop Reservoir, Calderdale Borough.

Evidence of a once forested land, the only remaining dead tree on the moors to be found in the area, very symbolic of the title 'Forgotten Landscape', close to the summit of the very windswept Stiperden Moor (479m), Burnley Borough. OPPOSITE - A dry peat bog at The Clattering Stones, Widdop Moor, just over the Pendle boundary in Calderdale.

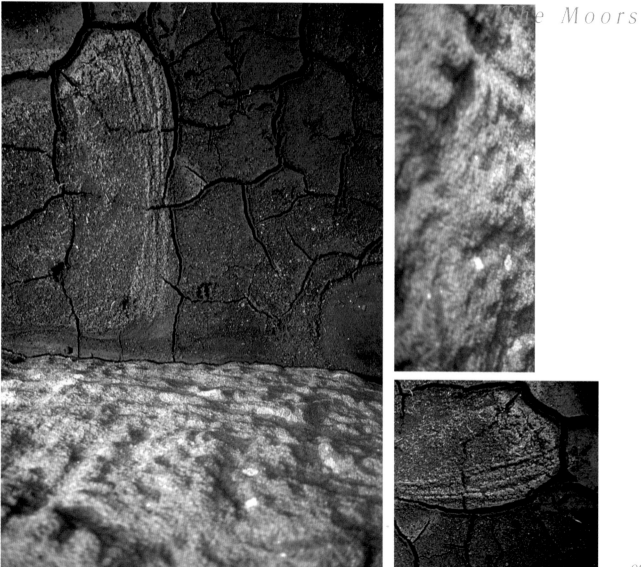

FORGOTTEN
images of Pendle Hill, the Ribble Valley and the Burnley area
LANDSCAPE

360 degree panorama looking across Deerstone & Red Spa Moors, Upper Coldwell Reservoir and Pendle Hill on the far left horizon, Pendle Borough.
LEFT - Waymarkers for the old pack-horse roads that crossed the moors.

Through the fence to Worsthorne Moor, as seen from Long Causeway, Burnley Borough.

Worsthorne Moor in autumnal shades, as seen from Long Causeway, Burnley Borough.

FORGOTTEN
LANDSCAPE

Images of Pendle Hill, the Ribble Valley and the Burnley Area

The twenty-four turbine Coal Clough Wind Farm, Burnley Borough. Eyesore or attraction?

LEFT - 'Potato Sacks', gritstone shaped by the wind and rain at the Bridestones.
ABOVE - A rainbow from the 'Blocks & Boulders' area, the Bridestones.
A frozen bog at the Bridestones' summit, 437m, Calderdale Borough.

FORGOTTEN
images of Pendle Hill, the Ribble Valley and the Burnley area
LANDSCAPE

Slag-heaps from an industrial age gone by, found near Hurstwood Reservoir, Burnley Borough. Abandoned for over 100 years and now covered in plantlife. Human mining and quarrying excavations have unintentionally resulted in a startling part of the landscape.

Cumulus clouds skirt across the high average relief of Will Moor, Pendle Borough.

FORGOTTEN
LANDSCAPE

Images of Pendle Hill, the Ribble Valley and the Burnley area

ABOVE - Many lines of the undulating moors as viewed south from the summit of Boulsworth Hill (517m), early on a winter morning, Pendle Borough.
OPPOSITE - A small tarn on the summit of Boulsworth Hill - Two different perspectives of 'Little Chair Stones' approaching the summit of Boulsworth Hill on a frosty February morning.

Pastoral

cattle, drystone walls and patchwork fields

FORGOTTEN LANDSCAPE

Images of Pendle Hill, the Ribble Valley and the Burnley area.

Sheep grazing in the summertime at the foot of Pendle Hill.
ABOVE - The sun sets behind a drystone wall near Barley, Pendle Borough.

As mentioned in the introduction, the focus of this book (as you will appreciate by now) is about what occurs naturally; flora, to a lesser extent fauna and the ever-changing climatic conditions. The core of a landscape however is the geological formations that make the shape and structure of what we see. A huge part of the Forgotten Landscape is agricultural and hence an integral part of the type of scenery a visitor would expect to see. Indeed farming makes up so many features endemic to our own association with the landscape.

This alteration of the landscape by years of human endeavour, for, in the main, cattle farming dates back for many centuries. This has resulted in spectacular patchwork fields on gentle slopes and many features from rustic dry-stone walls to grazing sheep which are as important to the area's identity as the hills and moorlands themselves. The walls in particular often take on some improbable lines (up the 'Big End' of Pendle Hill for example), weaving up and down intricate cloughs or winding along the roadside.

Blacko Tower highlights this exposed summit, typical of the farmlands found in the Borough of Pendle. The tower was built in 1890 by an eccentric Yorkshire born grocer, "to assist

Silhouetted sheep at Witch's Quarry, Ribble Valley.

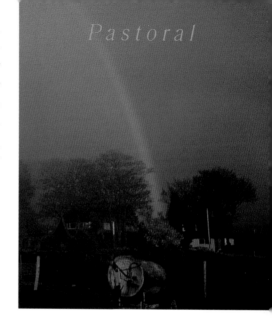

Pastoral

cattle, drystone walls and patchwork fields

I find the level of maintenance that farming brings to a landscape can highlight many of its features. The subtle aesthetics of the rolling countryside, the width of a valley or the drama of an exposed summit. The immaculately cut and trimmed farmlands of the Ribble Valley on the north side of Pendle Hill form a particularly picturesque landscape. Award winning stuff, although I'm almost afraid to breathe in case I knock a blade of grass out of place!

The farmlands also provide a network of walks; the Pendle, Brontë and Pennine Ways being the most famous. Stiles, kissing gates and steps in walls are found throughout the area's farms.

Although the prognosis for farming is an uncertain one, farming seems an enduring industry, and having survived the Foot & Mouth crisis in 2001, the future must surely be more optimistic?

There was once a huge billboard in a field which read '*Spectacular Countryside - Thanks to Farming*'. Well they've certainly got a point which this section of the book should help to prove!

ABOVE - Rainbow in a field near Gorple Road, Worsthorne, Burnley.
RIGHT - Abandoned farming machinery, Wycoller, Pendle Borough

FORGOTTEN
images of Pendle Hill, the Ribble Valley and the Burnley area
LANDSCAPE

The rolling green countryside of the Ribble Valley, looking towards Rimington from Downham Moor.

As seen from the main path of Pendle Hill in winter, the 296m lump of Barley Green being highlighted on the right, Pendle Borough.

FORGOTTEN LANDSCAPE

Images of Pendle Hill, the Ribble Valley and the Burnley Area

LEFT - 'Vaccary Walls' found throughout the area, but most famously at Wycoller, Pendle Borough.
ABOVE - Sheep at Wycoller.
PREVIOUS PAGE - Farming meets the moorland of Boulsworth Hill, Wycoller Country Park.

FORGOTTEN
LANDSCAPE

Images of Pendle Hill and the Ribble Valley and the Burnley area

LEFT - Sheep grazing on the moorland near Wycoller Country Park, Pendle Borough.
ABOVE - Birch trees divide the fields of the Ribble Valley, as seen from Clitheroe Road.

Newborn calves and mother at a farm in Worsthorne, Burnley Borough.

FORGOTTEN
LANDSCAPE

Images of Pendle Hill, the Ribble Valley and the Burnley area

LEFT - Pendle Side Farm in the snow, Pendle Borough.
ABOVE - Sheep feeding on a haystack on a cold winter morning, Pendle Side Farm.

A small herd of black cows grazing on Deerstone Moor, Pendle Borough.

FOLLOWING PAGE - Perhaps the most quintessential part of the pastoral landscape: the drystone wall. CLOCKWISE FROM LEFT - Widdop Reservior, Calderdale Borough - Swindon Reservoir, Burnley Borough - Wycoller, Pendle Borough - Barley village, Pendle Borough - Lane Bottom, Burnley Borough. OPPOSITE - on Pendle Hill.

FORGOTTEN LANDSCAPE

Images of Pendle Hill and the Ribble Valley and the Burnley area

Scenes from Wycoller Country Park,
Pendle Borough.

FORGOTTEN LANDSCAPE

The dark atmosphere of witch country captured by barbed wire near Barley village, Pendle Borough.

The coping stones of a drystone wall and a cirrus sky near Barley village, Pendle Borough.

Patchwork fields of Pendle Borough as seen from Earl's Crag - Lambs can be seen throughout the area in the spring time.

The undulating farmlands which surround the village of Barley, Pendle Borough.

The area's relative proximity to the coastline and the Irish Sea ensures spectacular sunsets are frequent events.
ABOVE - The pristine pastoral lands of the Ribble Valley as seen from Witches Quarry, Ribble Valley.

Reservoirs

Reeds, ducks, geese and calm waters

FORGOTTEN LANDSCAPE

Images of Pendle Hill, the Ribble Valley and the Burnley area

A moorhen enjoying the evening light on Foulridge Reservoir, Pendle Hill in background, Pendle Borough. ABOVE - A glowing horizon at Foulridge Reservoir.

The Forgotten Landscape covers a relatively small area of land, being situated in the North West of England it is of no surprise that the area receives one of the highest annual rainfalls in the UK. Consequently there are some twenty reservoirs within the Burnley and Pendle area supplying water to much of the North West of England.

Windsurfing at Cloughbridge Reservoir, Burnley Borough. BELOW - Canada geese fighting at Cant Clough Reservoir, Burnley Borough.

The reservoirs are of course an alteration of the landscape by human action, human necessity you could even say. Personally, I find they only embellish the landscape adding a burst of light and contrast in shape and colour to the norm. There is something very tranquil about walking alongside a large body of water, perhaps its being in the presence of such a large mass of one substance that lies totally still and silent that one finds so humbling? It is particularly surreal at first light.

The reservoirs also bring new wildlife to the landscape, fish, ducks, swans and geese being the primary examples. Frogs and even lizards are also present for the patient nature enthusiast. The massive array of insect life should also not go unmentioned from butterflies to beetles and of course the infamous midge. These swarming critters can turn a summer's evening by the lake into shear misery; clinical insanity is a real possibility if the appropriate repellents are not employed!

The reservoirs also bring new recreational opportunities to the area; sailing and canoeing at Clowbridge, Foulridge and Coldwell. Swimming is not recommended. The most popular past-time to be found around the reservoirs however is fishing.

Still waters for an early morning at Upper Black Moss Reservoir Pendle Borough. BELOW - Canada geese at Black Moss.

Upper Coldwell, Black Moss and Swinden Reservoirs being the best examples (permission/licence must be obtained first).

The reservoirs often come in pairs of upper and lower - Gorple, Foulridge, Ogden, Black Moss, Swinden, and Coldwell are all found in pairs, presumably this is a failsafe way of keeping the reserves of water topped up? The single reservoirs of - Widdop, Cant Clough, Churn Clough, Clowbridge, Walverden, Whitemoor, Higherford, Hurstwood and Clough Bottom also have their own special charm.

The reservoirs bring a great sense of peace in contrast to the busy urban and industrial corridor. They are the choice of those in pursuit of the more leisurely type of activity as there is one thing that the walks around all the reservoirs have in common, although distances vary dramatically, they are all flat! This final section of the book will add to the existing appreciation of one of the real bonus features to the Forgotten Landscape.

FORGOTTEN
LANDSCAPE

Images of Pendle Hill and the Ribble Valley and the Burnley area

Willow trees on the eastern shores of Foulridge Reservoir, Pendle Borough.

Canada geese flying over Cant Clough Reservoir, Burnley Borough.
LEFT - Reeds at Foulridge Reservoir, Pendle Borough.

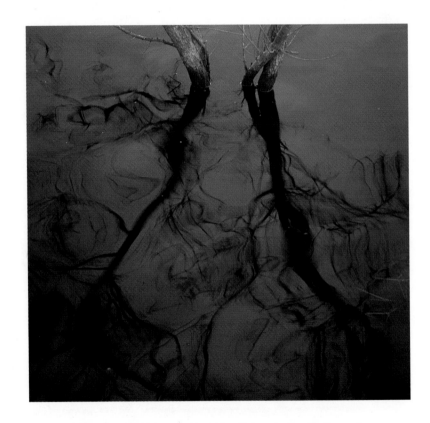

Willow trees in the water, Foulridge Reservoir, Pendle Borough.
OPPOSITE - Panoramic scenes from Lower Foulridge Reservoir.

Upper Coldwell Reservoir situated on Red Spa Moor, Pendle Borough, Pendle Hill in background.

A moody sky over Widdop Reservoir, Calderdale Borough.
OPPOSITE - Cant Clough Reservoir, Burnley Borough - Widdop Reservoir as seen from The Clattering Stones, Calderdale Borough - A sturdy drystone wall by Upper Swinden Reservoir, Burnley Borough.

FORGOTTEN
LANDSCAPE

The picturesque Widdop Reservoir just over the Pendle boundary in Calderdale Borough. The gritstone rock buttresses and boulders popular with climbers can be seen on the top right horizon.

FORGOTTEN
LANDSCAPE
images of Pendle Hill, the Ribble Valley and the Burnley area

Conifer trees reflect in Hurstwood Reservoir, Burnley Borough.
LEFT - Waymarker for the Pennine Bridleway, Hurstwood. INSET - Overview of Hurstwood Reservoir.

The tranquility of Upper Black Moss Reservoir, early on a spring morning, Pendle Borough.
OPPOSITE - Inlet of the reservoir - Pendle Hill makes the perfect backdrop - Barley conifer forest reflected in the calm waters - Reeds in the water make a perfect nesting habitat for ducks, geese and frogs.

Black Moss Reservoirs (upper & lower) as seen from Pendle Hill's main path in mid summer, Pendle Borough.
The upper reservoir was first constructed in 1912.

Black Moss Reservoirs (upper & lower) as seen from Pendle Hill's summit at sunset, Pendle Borough.

FORGOTTEN LANDSCAPE
Images of Pendle Hill, the Ribble Valley and the Burnley area

A mallard duck (female) on frozen surface water.
OPPOSITE - Churn Clough Reservoir near Sabden at the foot of Spence Moor,
Ribble Valley/Pendle Boundary.

The sun sets over Widdop Reservoir, Calderdale Borough.

Acknowledgements

By the same author -

Eyes Up - a pictorial odyssey of life and landscape through a climber's lens (Posing Productions 2002).
Climbing New Zealand - a crag guide for the travelling rock climber (Posing Productions 2000).
OZ Rock - a rock climber's guide to Australian crags (Cicerone Press 1997).

Forgotten Landscape - images of Pendle Hill, the Ribble Valley and the Burnley area, first edition 2003.

Published by Posing Productions, Burnley, Lancs, UK - www.posingproductions.com

All photographs are Copyright © Alastair Lee 2003

All photographs, design and graphics, text and captions by Alastair Lee.

ISBN - 0-9541382-2-8

Printed and bound at the De Montfort Press by Raithby, Lawrence & Company Limited, UK.

Acknowledgements

A special thanks goes to the following people who've all been extremely helpful with the production of this book, from picture editing, layout ideas and proof reading to general encouragement, I would like to personally thank the following people - Richard and Jane Davies of Dysons Arts, Nelson - Ian Brockbank of Badger Books, Burnley - the ever supportive Valerie Le Clerc - Mum & Dad.

Many, many thanks to all the sponsors who get a special mention on the opposite page, without their financial assistance this book would not exist.

Further Reading
For more information about walking, accommodation or the history of the Burnley & Pendle area please visit
www.pendletourism.com